18.19

AN ILLUSTRATED GUIDE TO
S⚽CCER

A game of strength and soul...

HISTORY

Soccer is the world's most popular sport. Although ball-kicking games can be traced as far back as ancient Greece and China, modern soccer originated in England, in the 19th century. The Football Association laid down the first set of rules in 1863, and the first organized league was established in 1888. Carried outside Britain by sailors and expatriates, the game quickly caught on in the rest of Europe, South America, and Asia. The Fédération Internationale de Football Association (FIFA), the world's official governing body, was founded in 1904, with headquarters in Paris (later moved to Zurich). Soccer became an Olympic sport in the Olympic Games of 1908. In 1930 FIFA organized the World Cup, a tournament contested every four years to determine international soccer supremacy.

The World Cup is the most coveted price in soccer. The tournament, which lasts a month, culminates more than two years of qualifying play in six world regions. A total of 204 nation teams entered the competition in 2010, of which 32 qualified for the final tournament. More than 3.4 billion television viewers watched one or more of the matches played in South Africa 2010, in which Spain defeated Netherlands to capture its first trophy. World Cup competition for women began in 1991, with tournaments also held every four years. The United States has won twice.

RULES OF THE GAME

Soccer is played according to the same basic rules all around the world, written an passed down by its regulating organization, FIFA.

The field, or pitch, is rectangular in shape, measuring 100–130 yards (91–119 meters) long and at least 50 yards (46 meters) wide. Each team is formed by 11 players, including the goalkeeper. The goalkeeper is the only player who may touch the ball with the hands or arms, and only within a designated area. The other players attempt to advance the ball by kicking, or sometimes heading it to a teammate. The object is to force the ball into the opponent's goal —24 feet (7.3 meters) wide and 8 feet (2.4 meters) high— at the far end of the field. In official competitions, a match lasts 90 minutes, played in 45 minutes halves.

Combining speed, skill, and chess like strategy, soccer attracts numerous players and spectators throughout the world. Professional clubs play in domestic leagues before passionate crowds. Concurrent with league play, top clubs may compete in annual continent-wide tournaments, such as the European Champions League, or Copa Libertadores in South America.

In the United States, the growth of soccer has taken place largely at the amateur level —community youth leagues, high schools, and colleges— since the 1960's, U.S. professional leagues (mostly notably the North American Soccer League, 1966–84 and the present Major League Soccer) have had passing success.

Formation:

A team's alignment of players on the field. This is described with a set of three numbers, representative of the defenders, mid fielders, and forwards, that add up to 10. (The goalkeeper is not considered.) In a 4-4-2 formation, for example, there will be 4 defenders, 4 mid fielders, and 2 forwards. There is no restriction on a team's formation, and these change based on the game situation.

Goalkeeper:

The player responsible for stopping or blocking shots at his team's goal. The goalkeeper is also the only player allowed to use the hands, but his ability is limited to the penalty area. A keeper who touches the ball with the hands while outside the area risks a yellow card or even a red card.

Defenders:

The group of players whose primary duty is to prevent the opposition's attackers for scoring goals. Customarily defenders come in several positions, including center backs, right or left backs, and sweepers.

Midfielders:

The set of players who are equally responsible for defense and attack. Primary duties include winning the ball from the opposing team and creating scoring chances for their own team. The generic term covers a set of varying roles, including wingers, attacking mid fielders, and defensive mid fielders, among others.

Forwards:

The players who operate closest to the opposing goal, forwards are the most frequent goal scorers and play-makers; sometimes called strikers.

Goal area:

A box set within the larger penalty box, from which goal kick are taken by the defending team. The goal area extends six yards into the field of play.

muzsy / Shutterstock.com

Referee:

The official who judges and enforces the rules of the game. He or she is aided by two assistants whose primary responsibility is to determine offside infractions. A fourth official, on the sideline, supervises substitutions.

Goal:

The only kind of scoring play in soccer, worth one unit each. The entire ball must cross the goal line —the line underneath the crossbar that links the goalposts — to be counted as a goal. The goal itself is a rectangle 24 feet wide and eight feet high.

Own Goal:

When a defending player, normally by deflection, knocks the ball into his team's goal.

Goal Line:

The line that marks either end of the field. If the ball exits the field over the goal line, the result is either a corner kick (if last touched by the defending team) or a goal kick. If the entire ball crosses the goal line in the area surrounded by the goal structure, a goal is awarded. Outside of the goal, the goal line is often called simply the end line.

Goal Kick:

The kick that restarts play after the attacking team knock the ball over the end line. This kick is usually taken by the goalkeeper.

Arc:

The D-shaped line at the top of the penalty area. The line demarcates a circular distance of 10 yards from the penalty spot.

Card:

A disciplinary system available for the referee. The **YELLOW CARD** is shown for overly tough fouls or for persistent fouling by a single player. On violent fouls, the referee may choose to show a **RED CARD**, thereby expelling the offending player from the game. Two yellow cards shown to the same player during the course of a match, equal a red card.

Friendly:

An exhibition match

Time:

Game time of two 45 minute halves, usually counting up from zero, with stoppage time added at the end of each half.

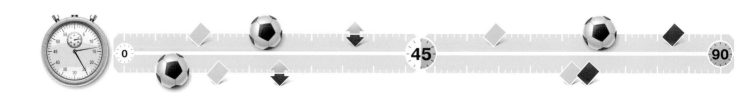

0   45   90

Stoppage Time:

The period of time at the end of either half to account for substitutions, injuries and time-wasting.

katatonia82 / Shutterstock.com

Extra Time:

An added 30-minute period of play, used only in some tournaments (such as the knockout stage of the World Cup) of the contest is tied after regulation. If there is no score after 30 minutes, the game is usually decided by a penalty shootout.

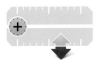

Free Kick:

The action that returns the ball to play after a foul. The victimized team is allowed a 10 yard circle free of enemy defenders. Near the opposing goal, a free kick offers a good shooting opportunity.

Ryu Voelkel

Penalty Kick:

The victimized team is given a free kick from the penalty spot with only the goalkeeper to beat.

Corner Kick:

A free kick taken from either corner of the field by the attacking team, awarded when the ball crosses the end line after being last touched by a defender. As with any free kick, the defending team must be at least 10 yards from the spot of the kick.

Shootout:

The act of taking alternating penalty kicks to decide a game. Each team receives five attempts (or more if the tie persists) from the penalty spot.

Penalty Box:

A box that begins 18 yards outside either goalpost, at right angles to the goal line, and extends 18 yards into the field of play. The penalty area has two rules attached. A goalkeeper may touch the ball with the hands while inside the box, and a foul on the attacking team inside the penalty area results in a penalty.

Penalty Spot:

A small circle 12 yards from the goal line, at the center of the box or penalty area, from which penalties are taken.

Substitutions:

In most league games, three substitutions per game (per team) are permitted. The player removed cannot return to the match. In friendly matches, usually only five substitutions are permitted, though this limit may be raised with the agreement of both teams.

Throw In:

The action that restarts play after the ball goes over the touchline. The player grasps the ball with two hands and throws it back onto the field.

Touchline:

The boundary that borders either side of the field. If the entire ball goes over the touchline, the team that did not touch the ball is awarded a throw in.

Halfway Line:

The line that divides the field in half across the center.

Offside:

An infraction at the moment the ball is passed by a teammate, and the offensive player does not have two opposing defenders (usually counting the goalkeeper as one) between him or her and the goal line. The attacker is considered offside, and that infraction awards a free kick for to the defending team.

Draw:

When the match is tied at game's end. In league play both team will receive one point in the standings.

Foul:

An infraction decided by the referee; usually given for body contact that does not touch the ball first. The fouled team is awarded a free kick.

Through Ball:

A pass that splits the opposing defense to an onrushing attacker; often used to describe passes that beat the offside trap.

Cross:

An attacking pass from either side of the field into the penalty area. Frequently aimed at the heads of forwards.

INTERNET RESOURCES

www.fifa.com

The Official Website of the 2014 FIFA World Cup Brazil™ and Fédération Internationale de Football Association (FIFA)

www.ussoccer.com

U.S. Soccer is the national governing body of the sport. Includes news, video, tournaments, coverage of all US National teams and information.

www.mlssoccer.com

The official site with news, standings, clubs, statistics, players and videos for the MLS.

www.womensprosoccer.com

Official home of Women's Professional Soccer. Find information about WPS soccer players, teams, games and headline sports news.

sportgraphic Shutterstock.com

Mason Crest

370 Reed Road
Broomall, PA 19008
www.masoncrest.com

Author: Paco Elzaurdia

Photo credits:
Used under license from Shutterstock, Inc.: 1-32

ISBN-13: 978-1-4222-2669-8
E-Book ISBN: 978-1-4222-9210-5

Cataloging-in-Publication Data on file with the Library of Congress